Earth

BY MARION DANE BAUER
ILLUSTRATED BY JOHN WALLACE

Ready-to-Read

Simon Spotlight
New York London Toronto Sydney New Delhi

For my grandson, Cullen Bauer-Trottier,
with love —M. D. B.

To Phoebe —J. G. W.

SIMON SPOTLIGHT

An imprint of Simon & Schuster Children's Publishing Division
1230 Avenue of the Americas, New York, New York 10020
This Simon Spotlight edition December 2021
Text copyright © 2021 by Marion Dane Bauer
Illustrations copyright © 2021 by John Wallace
SIMON SPOTLIGHT, READY-TO-READ, and colophon are registered
trademarks of Simon & Schuster, Inc.
For information about special discounts for bulk purchases, please contact
Simon & Schuster Special Sales at 1-866-506-1949 or
business@simonandschuster.com.
Manufactured in the United States of America 1021 LAK
2 4 6 8 10 9 7 5 3 1
Library of Congress Cataloging-in-Publication Data
Names: Bauer, Marion Dane, author. | Wallace, John, 1966– illustrator.
Title: Earth / Marion Dane Bauer ; [illustrated by] John Wallace.
Description: New York, New York : Simon Spotlight, 2021. | Series: Our
universe | Summary: "Learn all about planet Earth in the third book in this
nonfiction Level 1 Ready-to-Read series about the universe that's perfect for
kids who love science and space!"— Provided by publisher.
Identifiers: LCCN 2021028927 | ISBN 9781534486485 (paperback) |
ISBN 9781534486492 (hardcover) | ISBN 9781534486508 (ebook)
Subjects: LCSH: Earth (Planet)—Juvenile literature.
Classification: LCC QB631.4 .B38 2021 | DDC 525—dc23
LC record available at https://lccn.loc.gov/2021028927

Glossary

✦ **amoebas** (say: ah-ME-bahs): tiny living things made of only one cell.

✦ **atmosphere** (say: at-MUH-sfir): the envelope of air surrounding a planet.

✦ **erupt**: to release or burst suddenly and violently against restraint.

✦ **Goldilocks zone** (say: GOAL-dee-locks zohn): in the story *The Three Bears*, Goldilocks found one porridge too hot, another too cold, and the third just right. A planet is in the "Goldilocks zone" when it is not too hot or too cold—just the right temperature for life.

✦ **scientists** (say: SIE-uhn-tists): people who observe and do research or experiments in a particular area of interest to better understand the world around us.

✦ **tilt**: to tip, lean, or slant.

✦ **water bears**: creatures so tiny they can only be seen through a microscope. They have four pairs of stout legs, and they usually live in water or damp moss. Their scientific name is "tardigrade." They are also called "moss piglets."

✦ **water vapor** (say: WAH-tuhr VAY-puhr): water as a gas instead of a liquid.

Note to readers: Some of these words may have more than one definition. The definitions above match the ways these words are used in this book.

Earth is a lucky planet.
It is just the right
distance from the Sun.

Sun

Not too hot.
Not too cold.
Scientists call this
the **Goldilocks zone!**

Goldilocks zone

Earth

Each time Earth spins,

you wake up to a new day.

Each time Earth travels
around the Sun,

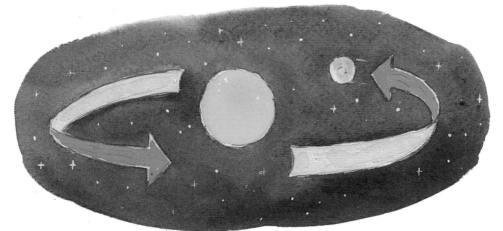

you turn one year older.

Earth has a special **tilt**
that gives us seasons.

The part that tips toward
the Sun warms into summer.

The part that tips away
cools into winter.

When Earth was born,
it was so hot, everything
was melted rock.

As it cooled, a crust formed.
Then volcanoes **erupted**
through the crust!

The volcanoes gave off **water vapor** and gases, forming our oceans and **atmosphere**.

Earth is the only planet we
know that supports life.

Life on Earth can be
as tiny as **amoebas**
or **water bears**,

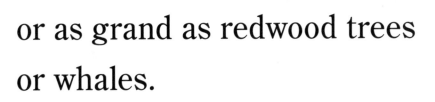

or as grand as redwood trees
or whales.

It can be as musical
as birds,

or as silent as fish.

Life on Earth can be
as sweet as a rose,

or as stinky as a skunk.

Or as stinky as
skunk cabbage!

You are part of
life on Earth too!

We humans are newcomers
to this world,

but we live
all around the globe.

We live in forests,

beside oceans,

in cities,

and on farms.

We speak different languages
and have different customs.

We wear different clothes

and live in different kinds
of homes.

But we are all children
of this Earth.

We must take care of our
home every day
of our lives.

Interesting Facts

✦ The Earth is more than four-and-a-half billion years old.

✦ The Sun is ninety-three million miles from our Earth. It takes eight minutes for light to travel from the Sun to us.

✦ Although we cannot feel the movement, we are zooming around the Sun at the amazing speed of eighteen-and-a-half miles per second!

✦ Many different factors make life as we know it possible on our planet. One is oxygen in our atmosphere. Another is the presence of water. And another is the temperature's being "just right." Earth's atmosphere gathers and holds the Sun's heat. Without our atmosphere, the temperature would be zero degrees all the time.

Climate Change

✦ Our planet is always changing, but humans are changing it faster than ever before. Burning fossil fuels and cutting down forests create big problems with our climate.

✦ Governments must work to solve these problems, but every person can help. We can plant trees. Trees store carbon and give back oxygen. We can use water with care. All life needs water. We can recycle to keep trash from our oceans and our land. And we can learn more about the climate crisis. All of these actions help care for the planet we call home.